3

Cr
—
En

THE GROLIER
STUDENT
ENCYCLOPEDIA
OF ■*SCIENCE* ■*TECHNOLOGY AND THE* ■*ENVIRONMENT*

Grolier Educational Corporation
SHERMAN TURNPIKE, DANBURY, CONNECTICUT, 06816

Acknowledgments

The author and publishers are grateful to the following for permission to reproduce copyright photographs:

Cover photograph: Coo-ee Picture Library

Argyle Diamond Mines, p. 21 (left); Austral International, p. 55 (left); Brian Chudleigh/A.N.T. Photo Library, p. 44 (right); Coo-ee Picture Library, pp. 19 (right), 20, 32, 52 (left), 57; Steve Hicks/A.N.T. Photo Library, p. 34; Horizon International, p. 29; International Photographic Library, p. 21 (right); Kathie Atkinson, pp. 6 (top), 7 (top), 8 (left), 16 (right), 31, 36, 46, 56 (top), Dale Mann/Retrospect, p. 51 (bottom), 55 (right); The Mansell Collection, p. 62; NASA, pp. 39, 42, 48; Oceaneering Australia Pty. Ltd., p. 28 (right); The Photo Library, p. 9; C. & S. Pollitt, p. 35 (bottom), 38 (bottom); Otto Rogge/A.N.T. Photo Library, p. 24; Peter Stannard, p. 8 (right); Silvestris/A.N.T. Photo Library, p. 17 (top); Stock Photos, pp. 5, 10, 11, 12, 13 (top), 14, 15, 16 (left), 17 (bottom), 18, 27, 33, 34, 35 (top), 27, 38 (top), 41, 53, 54, 59, 60, 61.

Published by Grolier Educational Corporation 1996
Edited and updated by Grolier Educational Corporation 1996
Copyright © Macmillan Education Australia Pty Ltd 1995

Cataloging Information can be obtained from Grolier Educational Corporation

Set ISBN: 0-7172-7517-5

Set in Garamond by Superskill Graphics, Singapore
Printed in Singapore

Contributors

Writers

Jan Anderson BSc (Hons), MSc
Glenn Beattie BEd, DipT, GCertEd
Nigel Bennett BEd (Hons)
Harry Breidahl BSc (Ed)
Diana Chase BA, TC
Robin C. Glenie FRMIT (Geology by Research)
Angela Hehir BAgSc, DipEd, BND
Robin Hirst BSc (Hons), PhD, DipEd
Sally Hirst BEd (Hons)
Graham Houghton BA (Hons)
Jim Howes TPTC, BA
Valerie Krantz BA, DipLibSt, TC
Stephen Ray BSc
Frank Ryan BA, DipT
Gill Shannon BSc (Hons)
John Wilkinson BSc, DipEd, MAIP, DipEdAdmin

Editors

Stephen Dobney
Anita Gray
Sally Green
Kate Lovett
Ruth Ridgway

Illustrators

Warren Crossett
Paul Konye
Xiangyi Mo
Doug Pitt
Doug Priestly

Crocodiles and Alligators

Crocodiles and alligators are reptiles with long bodies, short legs, webbed feet, and very thick hides. They have strong jaws and teeth. Alligators have a broad snout, but crocodiles have a narrower, pointy snout, and two of their lower teeth stick out when the jaws are closed.

The eyes, ears and nostrils of crocodiles and alligators are on the top of their heads. This means they can lie in the water with just the top of their heads showing and still be on the lookout for prey. They use their flattened tails as weapons, and as rudders when they are swimming.

Habitat

Crocodiles and alligators are found mostly in tropical parts of the world. The American crocodile, and the saltwater crocodile of southern Asia and northern Australia, both grow up to 23 feet (7 meters) long. They may weigh up to 1 ton (1 tonne). The American alligator can grow to 13 feet (4 meters).

Crocodiles live in lairs dug out of the banks of rivers and lakes. The entrance to the lair is underwater. They usually eat fish, but will eat other animals.

The alligator (top) has a broader snout than the crocodile (bottom).

Breeding

Usually, crocodiles lay 30 to 60 eggs at a time. Most species bury their eggs at the edge of the water and leave them to hatch. The Nile crocodile digs a nest for the eggs, and both parents look after the young for about two months.

Male alligators below loudly and often fight during the mating season. The female alligator lays her eggs in a nest made from branches and rotting plant matter. She stays near the nest until the eggs hatch. The baby alligators leave the nest and fend for themselves as soon as they emerge.

A freshwater crocodile in Australia's Northern Territory.

The American alligator lives in the swamps of the southeastern United States.

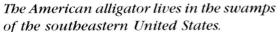

Crocodiles and Alligators

Danger to humans

The saltwater crocodile will attack humans. Alligators are not likely to attack humans.

The skin trade

Crocodiles and alligators were once widely hunted for their skins to make items such as shoes and handbags. Most species are now protected, but in some places there are special farms where crocodiles are raised for their skins.

Saltwater crocodiles can grow up to 23 feet (7 meters) long and weigh up to one ton (one tonne).

Crocodiles and Alligators - See also: *Dinosaurs, Endangered Animals, Prehistoric Animals, Reptiles.*

A saltwater crocodile hatching from its egg.

 **c**

Crustaceans

There are more than 30,000 species of crustaceans. Crabs, lobsters, shrimps, barnacles and water fleas are all crustaceans. Most live in the sea and have a hard shell covering their body. Some species live in fresh water. A few, such as woodlice, live in moist areas on land. Crustaceans come in many sizes, from tiny water fleas to crabs with a leg span of 10 feet (3 meters).

Crustaceans are invertebrates. The shell of a crustacean is its skeleton. In order to grow, a crustacean has to shed its shell several times during its life. A new shell grows under the old one, but it is soft at first, and the animal

Shrimp have long limbs to catch food.

The male fiddler crab has a huge claw to attract females.

Crystal

hides until it hardens to avoid being eaten by a predator. The hermit crab has a soft abdomen. It lives in, and carries about, a hollow object such as a mollusc's empty shell.

The body of most crustaceans is made up of three main parts: the head, the thorax and the abdomen. All crustaceans have two pairs of feelers on their heads. Most crustaceans have more than five pairs of limbs. Crabs usually have four pairs of legs and a pair of big claws for fighting and catching food.

Most crustaceans hatch from eggs. Crabs and lobsters look like tiny adults from the time they are born, but some crustaceans hatch as larvae that look very different from the adults. They change to the grown-up form later.

Woodlice live in moist areas on land, for example, under logs.

Crystal

Crystals are natural substances that form into solid shapes with a number of flat sides. Quartz is a mineral that commonly occurs in crystal form. Other crystals include precious stones such as diamonds and rubies.

The word 'crystal' comes from a Greek word meaning 'clear ice'. In the 17th century it was thought that clear quartz crystals were actually ice that had been hardened by a long and intense cold period. Later it was discovered that the regular shape of a crystal was related to the regular way the atoms making up the substance were arranged.

There are six basic types of crystals, each with a different shape. From the crystal structure of a substance, scientists can tell other things, such as its hardness and ability to conduct heat.

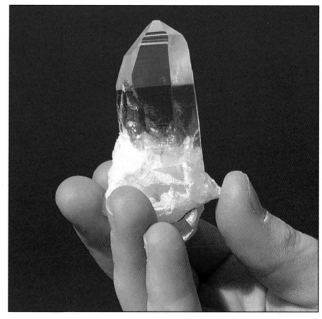

A large quartz crystal.

Crustaceans - See also: *Marine Animals.*

Crystal - See also: *Atom, Carbon, Diamond, Metal, Mineral, Precious Stones.*

Cc

Cyclones and Hurricanes

A cyclone is a low-pressure zone in the lower atmosphere in which winds spiral inwards. Some cyclones cover an area a few hundred miles across. Intense cyclones that are only a few hundred feet across are called tornadoes.

The atmospheric pressure is lowest in the center of a cyclone. In the Northern Hemisphere cyclone winds blow anticlockwise. In the Southern Hemisphere, cyclone winds blow clockwise. Storms are often associated with cyclones. However, not all cyclones bring bad weather. It depends on the type of air in the cyclone. For example, if a cyclone forms in dry air, there may not even be any clouds.

Tropical cyclones form over warm ocean waters in the tropics. Such cyclones usually cause much damage to places in the tropics. Cyclones that form in the West Indies or the eastern Pacific Ocean are called hurricanes. Cyclones that occur in the western Pacific Ocean are called typhoons. These storms bring winds up to 180 miles (290 kilometers) per hour and much rain, thunder and lightning. They are between 125 and 185 miles (200 and 300 kilometers) in diameter.

Cyclones are often seen on weather satellite photographs as tight, spiraling masses of white cloud. They are at their strongest when at sea. Once over land they tend to lose some of their intensity. However, they cause most damage when they pass over coastal towns.

> **Cyclones and Hurricanes** – See also: *Atmosphere, Barometer, Clouds, Hemisphere, Meteorology, Satellites, Storm, Weather, Wind*.

A tornado is a small intense cyclone.

Dairy Industry

Dairy products include milk, cheese, ice cream and butter. These products are made from cow's milk. However, some products come from the milk of goats and deer. Today there are more than 200 million cows around the world providing milk to make dairy products. The world's major dairy industries are in the United States, Australia, New Zealand and Europe.

Milk-producing animals were probably first kept in Asia. The idea spread to Europe as explorers brought back some of these animals. The cow became the main milk producer because it is very efficient at producing milk. Dairy farms gradually

The automatic milking machine was invented in the 19th century.

Making cheese in a dairy factory.

The process of pasteurization, invented by Louis Pasteur, kills harmful bacteria in milk.

increased in rural areas as populations grew. Improved transportation meant that milk could be quickly carried from rural farms to cities. This increased demand for milk and production stepped up.

Milk

All mammals receive milk as their first food. It provides protein, fat, carbohydrates and vitamins. These substances are important for the growth and formation of bones and teeth. Until the 19th century, farmers milked cows by hand. Today cows are milked by automatic milking machines. The machine is made up of a series of vacuum-powered suction cups. A clump of cups is attached to the cow's udders and the milk drawn out by suction and squeezing. Using this method, a healthy cow could produce up to 880 gallons (4,000 liters) of milk in one year.

Once fresh milk is collected, it has to be cooled to prevent the growth of bacteria. Refrigerated tankers carry it to the dairy factory. At the dairy, the milk is 'pasteurized' to destroy bacteria. The process of **pasteurization** was named after the French chemist, Louis Pasteur, who invented it. The process involves heating the milk to about 158°F (70°C) for 15 to 20 seconds before cooling it rapidly. This keeps the milk fresh longer. To prevent other bacteria from making the milk go sour, it is sterilized with steam for about 20 minutes. The sterilized milk passes through a vacuum chamber where the steam evaporates, leaving behind the milk. The milk is then packaged and sent to the shops.

Homogenized milk is forced through very small openings to break up the lumps of fat. The liquid is stirred to produce a uniform blend of milk fats (cream) and the thinner skim milk. To separate cream from skim milk, the milk is heated, then spun in a centrifuge. The cream is lighter and stays near the center of the spinning container. The skim milk and cream are marketed and sold separately.

Butter is made from cream. The cream in rotated in huge stainless steel drums until the butterfat particles form and clump together. Salt is added to prolong the life of the butter.

Cheese is made by turning milk sour with the addition of bacteria and rennet, an enzyme from calves' stomachs. This turns the milk into a curd. Heating produces a liquid (whey) that is drained off, leaving the curds. The curds are cut and pressed into cheese molds.

Dairy Industry – See also: *Cattle, Diet, Food, Food Preservation.*

Dam

A dam is a structure built across a waterway to hold the flow of water for storage. Dams are built to supply water for agriculture, domestic supply, or hydro-electricity.

The earliest known dam was built on the River Nile, about 3000 BC. It was made of stone and was about 50 feet (15 meters) high. Archaeologists have found the remains of several dams, built more than 2,000 years ago.

In the early days, a good dam was one that stayed up and held water. However, as long ago as 500 BC, Byzantine workers used a dam design that had a wall that curved upstream. This made the wall stronger and is still a feature of dams built today.

With the invention of different pieces of machinery, larger dams could be built. Modern dams built in mountains or narrow gorges are usually made of concrete. The

The Gordon River in Tasmania, Australia, was dammed to built a hydroelectric power station.

An embankment dam.

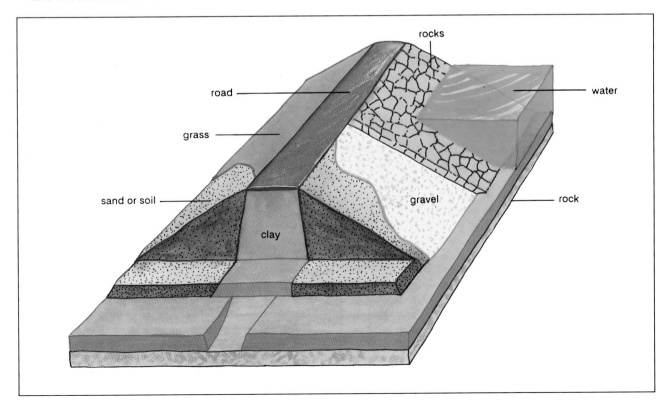

The Hoover Dam in the United States.

walls are curved (arched) so as to deflect the pressure of the water load against the sides of the mountains they are built between. Concrete dams are also thicker at their base. By sloping out towards the water load, the weight is deflected from pushing sideways directly on the wall to pushing downwards, onto the dam's stronger foundations. These are called gravity dams. The high pressure created by the water in these dams can be released to turn turbines that generate electricity. This power is called hydroelectric power.

Where dams are built across wide rivers, a triangular wall of rock and clay is used (embankment design). Both sides of these dams slope outwards from the top, so the triangle is thickest at the base where the water pressure is greatest. The center of the wall is made of clay. Rock is laid over the wall to protect the dam from erosion.

Dam - See also: *Cement and Concrete, Engineering, Hydroelectric Power, Water Energy, Water Supply.*

Day and Night

We usually refer to **day** as the time when the Sun is shining on our part of the world. **Night** is the time when our part of the Earth is dark, or turned away from the Sun. But night is really part of the whole day. The length of a whole day is the time it takes the Earth to spin or rotate once on its axis. Each whole day begins at midnight. The hours from midnight to noon are the a.m. (before noon) hours. Those from noon to midnight are the p.m. (after noon) hours.

The sun appears to move across the sky because the Earth rotates on its axis. It takes nearly 24 hours for the Earth to rotate once. This rotation is from west to east. This causes the Sun to appear to move from east to west each day (the opposite way).

It is because the Earth rotates on its axis that day and night occur. As the Earth rotates, only one half of it faces the Sun at any one time. While one half is in sunlight, the other half is in darkness.

Day and night are not always of equal length. If the Earth's axis were straight up and down, there would be 12 hours of daylight and 12 hours of night. But the Earth's axis is not vertical — it is tilted at an angle of about 23 degrees, causing the length of day and night to vary. Two other things also determine the length of day and night. These are how far from the equator a place is, and the Earth's position around the Sun. The length of daylight changes during the year in all parts of the world.

The longest day in the Southern Hemisphere is December 21, while the shortest day is June 21. In the Northern Hemisphere the longest day is June 21 and the shortest day December 21. The length of daylight varies very little at the equator. At the North and South Poles there is six months of

daylight and six months of night.

A solar day is the length of time that it takes the Earth to turn around once with respect to the Sun.

A business day is the number of hours of business in any one day.

Astronomers use a day called **sidereal** day. It is based on the period of the Earth's rotation as measured by fixed stars. This day equals 23 hours 56 minutes and 4 seconds of mean solar time.

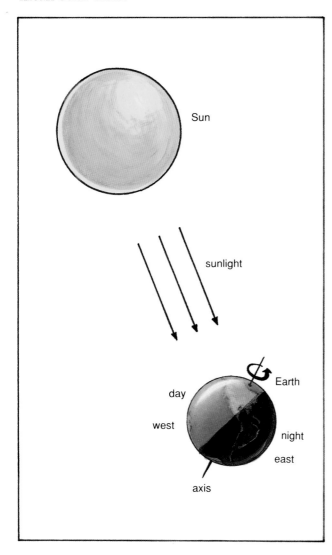

While half of the Earth is in sunlight, the other half is in darkness.

Day and Night - See also: *Calendar, Clock, Earth, Hemisphere, Moon, Solar System, Sun.*

Dentistry

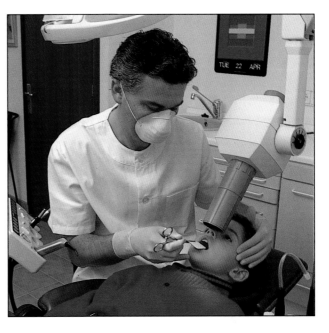

A dentist takes X-rays of a patient's teeth.

Dentistry is the science of caring for oral (mouth) tissues — the teeth and supporting bones, the gums and soft tissues. Diseases of the teeth, particularly dental caries (decay of the teeth) can be prevented by a good diet with reduced sugar, and the use of fluoride.

People under 35 years of age mostly lose teeth from dental caries. These teeth can often be repaired. People over 35 mostly lose teeth from gum disease, which can be prevented.

There are several specialty areas of dentistry. Orthodontics focuses on correcting the position of teeth. Periodontics concentrates on the care of the gums.

Dental schools are usually attached to medical schools, and a university degree is usually necessary before a dentist can practice.

Dentistry - See also: *Diet, Medicine, Teeth.*

Desert

Deserts are places with extremely high or low temperatures and little or no water. Despite these conditions, many plants and animals have found ways of surviving in deserts.

As much as 10 percent of the Earth's surface could be classed as hot desert, and a further 10 percent could be classed as polar desert. Deserts exist on every continent except Europe.

Arid deserts are those that are hot and dry. Lack of rainfall is one reason why these deserts come about. The Atacama Desert in Chile has had periods of up to 40 years with no rain at all.

Human activities also cause areas to become deserts. The Sahara Desert in north Africa was once farmland. When the farms became unproductive, goats were herded there. The goats ate all the vegetation, allowing the topsoil to be blown away by the wind.

The water-holding frog lives under ground in Australian deserts, only coming out when it rains.

Rocky deserts are more common than sandy deserts.

Some deserts are simply vast areas of sand. More common are rocky deserts, where all the topsoil and sand has been blown away.

Desert animals

Desert animals all have special features that allow them to survive in harsh, dry environments with little water. Camels are a good example. The Arabian camel, or dromedary, has a single hump in which it stores fat. In the dry season, when food is hard to find, the camel can live off this stored energy.

Small animals such as gerbils, jerboas and kangaroo rats live in holes in the ground to escape the heat. In the hot season they only come out at night. They get most of their water from the plants they eat.

A few species of frogs are found in the Australian deserts. They are called water-holding frogs, and they only appear on the surface when it rains. As the water dries up, the frogs take in water through their skin until they are almost round, and burrow into the soft, damp sand. They produce a thin transparent coating all over their body to keep

the water in. The frogs then go into a kind of sleep that can last up to two years, or until it rains again.

Deserts are also home to other creatures, including snakes, lizards, tortoises, scorpions, spiders and insects.

Desert plants

Despite the harsh conditions, there are many plants that are able to survive in dry desert environments.

Succulent or 'juicy' plants, such as the cactus, survive by storing water. When it rains they expand to store rainwater in their stems. During dry periods this water is used up and the cactus shrinks back to its original shape.

Some desert plants grow long roots that may extend down for 65 feet (20 meters) in search of water. Others have leaves that can absorb moisture from night mists and fogs.

Natural rock sculptures carved by the wind in Monument Valley, Utah, in the United States.

The leaves of the Welwitschia absorb moisture from night-time mists and fogs.

Some long-living plants lose their leaves and almost completely die back during a drought. Other desert plants have very short life cycles. Following a period of rain, the plants grow, flower and produce seeds very quickly, then die. The seeds remain in the soil until the next heavy rain begins the process again.

Desert - See also: *Amphibians, Continent, Drought, Flood, Insects, Land Degradation, Lizards, Mammals, Nocturnal Animals, Plants, Reptiles, Rodents, Sand, Soil, Spiders.*

The Antarctic is a polar desert.

Camels live off the fat in their humps when food becomes scarce in the desert.

Dd

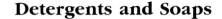

Detergents and Soaps

In soap-making, fats are boiled with caustic soda or potash in huge vats.

Detergents and soaps are chemical substances that are used to clean dirty surfaces. They are produced in the form of bars, flakes, granules, liquids and tablets. They have many uses in industry and in the home. People use soap to wash their bodies. Doctors clean sores and wounds with soap to kill germs that cause infection.

Soap is an ancient cleaner, dating back about 5,000 years. The first soap was a mixture of animal fats and wood ashes. Today soap is made from animal or vegetable fat mixed with a strong alkali such as caustic soda or potash. The mixes are boiled in tall vats. Salt water is added to the mixture to separate the soap from glycerine that also forms. The soap forms a sticky layer at the top of the vat. It is skimmed off and purified by further boiling. Colors and scents are then added.

Detergents are liquid or powder cleaning agents. Most detergents contain a synthetic **surfactant**. A surfactant makes water a more effective cleaner by making it 'wetter' — it reduces the surface tension of the water droplets, allowing the water to penetrate better. It pulls the dirt particles out of the material and holds them in the wash water until they are rinsed away. Substances such as bleaches, fabric softeners, and brighteners are also added to detergents. They are made in much the same way as soaps.

The technology of synthetic detergents came about as a result of the shortage of natural oils and fats during World War I. The petroleum industry now produces a wide range of synthetic detergents.

The main problem with detergents is that, unlike soaps, they do not break down easily in the environment. Many waterways have been ruined by detergent pollution.

Synthetic detergents can cause water pollution if they are not biodegradable.

Detergents and Soaps - See also: *Acids and Bases, Biodegradability, Pollution.*

Dew and Frost

Dew and frost are different forms of water that occur naturally in the environment.

Dew forms when the invisible water vapor present in the air **condenses** (forms droplets) on a surface. This happens when warm air, which has been heated by the Sun during the day, begins to cool at night. When the air comes into contact with a cool surface, droplets of dew form. Dew often forms on grass because the temperature is coolest at ground level. Dew also often forms on the inside of windows when the room temperature drops on a cold night.

Frost is frozen dew. It occurs in colder weather when the air is clear and very cold. As the temperature at ground level falls below freezing point, the dew turns to ice.

Frost is very damaging to new plants, and can be a serious problem for fruit and vegetable farmers. Plants affected by frost often turn black and may even die.

A serious condition called frostbite occurs when frost forms on the human body. This stops the blood flow and can even cause skin to die and drop off. People who live in cold parts of the world need to protect themselves against frostbite by covering their skin on very cold days or nights. Frost quickly turns back to water once the air temperature is above 32°F (0°C).

Dew is seen when water in the air condenses on a surface.

Dew and Frost – See also: *Air, Temperature.*

Dd

Diamond

Diamonds are crystals of pure carbon. They are the hardest substances known, and are quite rare. They range from colorless to black.

Diamonds are formed deep in the Earth's crust where the temperature and pressure are both very high. Volcanic activity brings them to the surface. Diamonds can also be made synthetically from graphite, another form of carbon. High pressure and temperatures of more than 5,500°F (3,000°C) are needed to turn the graphite into diamond.

Most diamonds that are mined are used in industry for drilling, cutting and polishing other hard materials, such as steel.

The highest quality diamonds are sold as gems. They are cut and polished to make them especially brilliant. Most diamonds used for gems are nearly transparent, or tinged with yellow or pink.

Australia is the world's biggest producer of diamonds. Zaire, Botswana, Russia and South Africa are also significant diamond-mining countries.

A gem-quality diamond before it is cut and polished.

Diamond - See also: *Carbon, Crystal, Precious Stones.*

Diet

Asian diets are high in rice and vegetables.

Diet describes all the food and drink a person consumes.

The body needs certain nutrients to grow normally. A lot of **macro-nutrients** are needed. They are mostly carbohydrates, proteins and fats, and they provide energy for the body to work. Proteins give the body amino acids, which repair body tissue and are important for growth. A small amount of **micro-nutrients** are also needed to help the body work properly. These include vitamins and minerals like calcium, iron and zinc. A good diet also includes plenty of dietary fiber and water.

Diseases can occur if not enough or too many of certain nutrients are included in a person's diet. Western diets are typically low in fiber; a lack of fiber can cause bowel complaints. People in Western countries also eat a lot of refined sugar which can cause dental decay.

Different cultures have different diets. Asian diets tend to use rice as the staple food. The

traditional Mediterranean diet uses wheat-based pastas, bread and semolina as the staple foods.

The word 'diet' is often used to describe an eating plan for people who want to lose weight. The safest way to lose excess weight is to have a sensible, long-term eating plan, lower in fat but containing all the nutrients the body needs, along with regular exercise. In Western cultures many young girls feel strong social pressure to be thin. This can lead to the serious condition of anorexia nervosa.

Carbohydrates, such as grains, fruits and vegetables, should form the main part of a balanced diet.

Diet – See also: *Cancer, Digestive System, Food, Food Preservation, Human Body*.

Digestive System

The digestive system is responsible for breaking food down into simpler substances. This means that nutrients are absorbed by the body, and solid waste is removed from the body. The digestive system is made up of a long muscular tube that starts at the mouth and ends at the anus. It includes the pharynx, esophagus, stomach, and small and large intestines. There are also large glands connected to the digestive system. These include the salivary glands in the mouth, the liver, the gall bladder and the pancreas; they release enzymes into the tube that help digestion. Enzymes are chemical substances made by the body.

Food is chewed in the mouth where the teeth and tongue physically break the food down into smaller pieces. The food is mixed with saliva to help in swallowing. Saliva also contains an enzyme to break the food into simple sugars.

The food then passes through the esophagus to the stomach. The stomach is a muscular organ that stores the food while it mixes it with an enzyme and other substances. Contractions of the stomach then send the food into the small intestine.

The small intestine digests and absorbs the food. It has a total length of about 20 feet (6 meters). The liver and pancreas send enzymes into the first part of the small intestine, called the **duodenum**. These enzymes break down the fats, proteins and carbohydrates so that the intestine can absorb them into the bloodstream. After digestion, the food becomes mostly fatty acids, simple sugars and amino acids. On the wall of the small intestine there are many **villi**, which look like little hairs. These help to absorb the food into the blood more quickly.

Food that is not digested goes from the small intestine to the large intestine. This becomes the waste material, or feces, and the large intestine re-absorbs a lot of the water in the feces. This water has come from the various substances in the intestine, as well as from the food itself. Bacteria break down the feces in the large intestine. From there, contractions move the feces along the large intestine to the anus, where they are excreted when a person goes to the toilet.

Digestive System – See also: *Diet, Food, Human Body, Liver, Teeth, Tongue*.

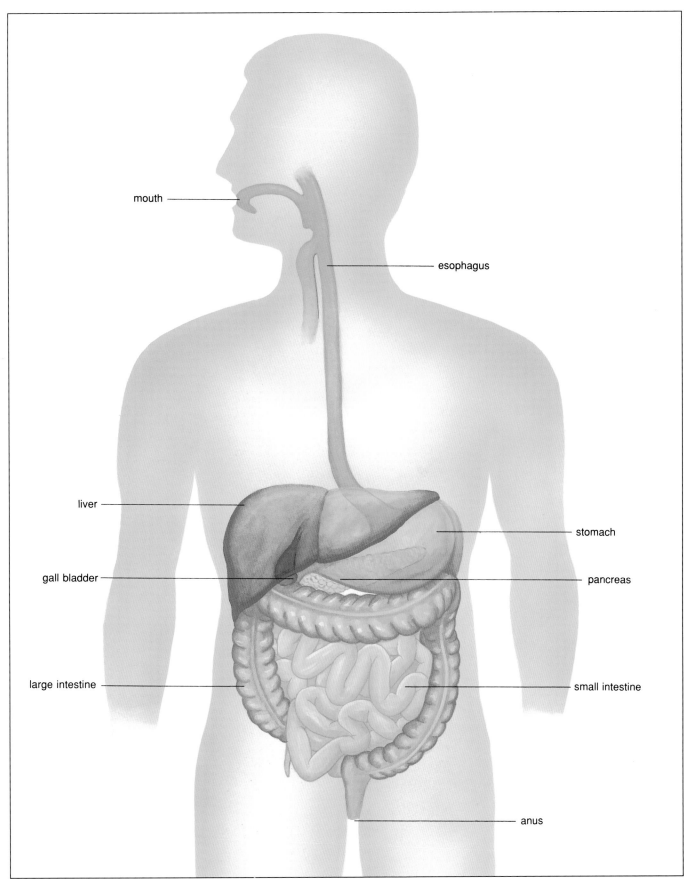

mouth

esophagus

liver

stomach

gall bladder

pancreas

large intestine

small intestine

anus

The digestive system.

Dinosaurs

Dinosaurs were large reptiles that lived on Earth between 220 million and 65 million years ago. The word 'dinosaur' means 'terrible lizard'. Fossils of more than 800 species of dinosaurs have been discovered so far, but more are being found.

The first dinosaurs

The first true dinosaurs walked on their hind legs, using their long tails for balance. Some were very heavy with a covering of bony armor. Others were light, with long necks and tails. They were all meat-eaters. Another group of dinosaurs evolved that had long necks and tails, and small heads with smaller teeth than the meat-eaters. These were plant-eaters.

Dinosaurs could move much faster than modern reptiles. Most are thought to have been cold-blooded. Some dinosaurs laid eggs, but others bore live young.

Dinosaurs rule the Earth

When the age of dinosaurs was at its height, about 140 to 190 million years ago, many types of dinosaurs increased in size. The plant-eaters were generally larger than the meat-

A rib bone from the Brachiosaur. Above the bone are models of the dinosaur and its skeleton, and a human model to give an idea of size.

eaters. *Diplodocus* weighed about 10 tons (10 tonnes) and reached a length of 90 feet (28 meters) with its long neck and whip-like tail. *Apatosaurus* (which used to be called *Brontosaurus*) was shorter, but weighed up to 30 tons (30 tonnes). The biggest one known so far, called *Supersaurus*, was about 100 feet (30 meters) high and weighed up to 100 tons (100 tonnes). These giant animals lived in herds, and probably spent a lot of time in swamps, feeding on the plants there. Plants grew very thick and lush in the warm and humid climate.

Meat-eating dinosaurs also increased in size. *Allosaurus* was 36 feet (11 meters) long. The meat-eaters could run twice as fast as the giant plant-eaters.

Not all dinosaurs were large, though. *Compsognathus* was only 2 feet (600 millimeters) long.

Two groups of dinosaurs lived in the sea. The ichthyosaurs looked a bit like dolphins, and the plesiosaurs looked like turtles.

The later dinosaurs

Over time, the continents drifted apart, the first flowering plants evolved, and dinosaurs gradually changed. *Tyrannosaurus*, the largest flesh-eating dinosaur, grew to be 40 feet (12 meters) long. Some of the small flesh-

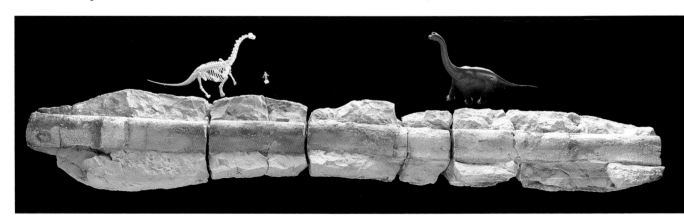

From left, Apatosaurus, Diplodocus and Allosaurus.

eaters, around 6 to 10 feet (2 to 3 meters) long, hunted in packs. Other dinosaurs evolved that looked like birds. They had long necks, toothless beaks, and long legs and fingers. They had a large brain compared with other dinosaurs. It is thought that they ate other dinosaurs' eggs and young dinosaurs.

The most successful of the plant-eating dinosaurs were the duck-billed dinosaurs, with their great grinding teeth for eating tough plant material such as pine needles. They had crests on top of their skulls and lived in herds in swamps and woodlands.

In 1979 a fossil dinosaur nursery was discovered. The fossil skeletons of 11 young dinosaurs were found in a hollow at the top of a nest mound that had been built of mud.

By 66 million years ago, the dinosaurs had all died out. Scientists are still not sure why they became extinct.

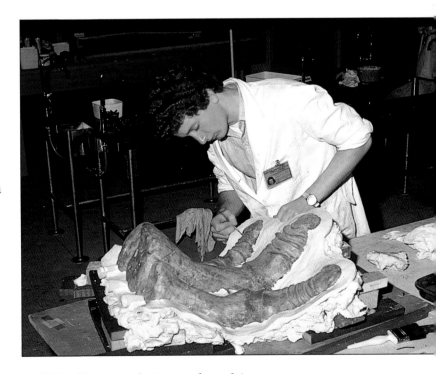

This dinosaur foot was found in many pieces, and had to be put together again.

Dinosaurs – See also: *Evolution, Fossils, Prehistoric Animals, Reptiles.*

Tyrannosaurus

meat-eater
49 ft (15 m)

Shantungosaurus

plant-eater
43 ft (13 m)

Parasaurolophus

plant-eater
33 ft (10 m)

Stegosaurus

plant-eater
30 ft (9 m)

Triceratops

plant-eater
30 ft (9 m)

Compsognathus

meat-eater
2 ft (0.6 m)

Oviraptor

meat-eater
6 ft (1.8 m)

*Dinosaurs came in many sizes. They are
classified according to the shape of their
hipbones. These dinosaurs did not all
live at the same time.*

Dd

Disease

Disease describes anything that affects the normal functioning of the body. The presence of disease may be obvious because of symptoms like fever, nausea or pain, or there may be no symptoms for a long time.

There are many causes of disease, and medical science is still learning about many of them. In the 19th century, Louis Pasteur linked micro-organisms to decay and fermentation. This helped scientists understand disease better. Then Robert Koch helped identify specific micro-organisms as the causes of specific diseases.

Safe water and better sanitation have helped to reduce the amount of infectious diseases in the 20th century. Antibiotics like penicillin, which destroy disease-making micro-organisms, were developed.

There are many types of diseases. Congenital diseases exist in a baby when it is born; they are often caused when something happens during pregnancy. The mother might drink too much alcohol, or the fetus may not develop normally for some other reason.

Metabolic diseases, like diabetes, occur when glands in the body do not work properly.

There are many infectious diseases. Infection by bacteria, fungi, protozoa, worms and viruses all have different effects on the body. AIDS is an infectious disease. Cancers are a group of diseases caused by body cells dividing abnormally, leading to tumors or growths.

Now, in the 20th century, many diseases that were serious in the past can be cured. Medical scientists can diagnose a disease more easily with the help of radiology and chemical analysis.

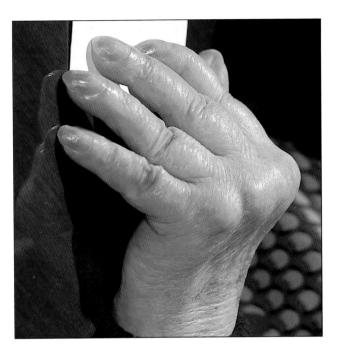

Arthritis is a disease that causes painful swelling of the joints.

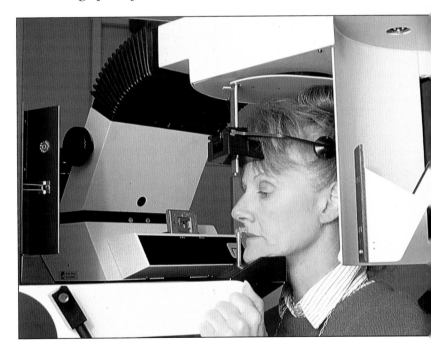

X-rays are an important tool in diagnosing disease.

Disease – See also: *Aging, AIDS, Antibiotics, Bacteria, Cancer, Diet, Doctor, Drugs, Infection, Medicine, Micro-organisms, Penicillin, Ultraviolet Radiation, Vaccination, Virus, Vitamins, X-rays.*

Diving

Divers often stay under water for long periods of time. They need a constant supply of fresh air. They also need a way of stopping themselves from floating up to the surface.

Below 130 to 165 feet (40 to 50 meters), the human body needs protection to withstand the water pressure. Also, if a person is in the water for too long, hypothermia (lowering of the body temperature) can cause death.

Deep-sea divers wear a protective suit that allows them to remain at surface pressure. These suits are called atmospheric diving systems (ADS) and are similar to the Manned Maneuvering Units worn by astronauts.

Divers in these suits can remain underwater for 72 hours at a depth of 2,300 feet (700 meters). They can move vertically and horizontally and use hand-gripped manipulators to complete tasks underwater, such as working on a wreck for long periods of time.

The word 'scuba' is an acronym for Self-Contained Underwater Breathing Apparatus. Scuba divers wear a wetsuit and carry their own air supply in tanks called aqualungs. They wear a weight belt and flippers. Scuba suits are widely used for commercial underwater projects and for scientific study. Scuba diving is also popular as a pleasure activity.

The WASP diving suit can stay underwater for 72 hours at a depth of 2,300 feet (700 meters).

Diving – See also: *Underwater Exploration.*

Dd

DNA

DNA stands for deoxyribonucleic acid. It is a molecule found in the nuclei of cells. DNA is the main component of chromosomes and has been described as the building block of life. It contains genetic information called **genes**, which determine such things as hair color and height. It can be artificially altered.

The structure of DNA was discovered in the early 1950s by two English scientists, James Watson and Francis Crick. It is considered one of the greatest discoveries in biological history.

The DNA molecule is in the shape of two spirals called **helixes**, which are mirror images of each other.

When new cells are formed, by splitting in two, each new cell receives one of the spirals so the genetic information is transferred. After cell division, the spirals make copies of themselves ready for the next division.

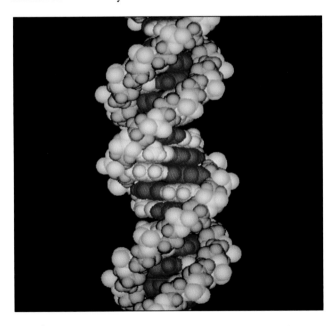

The DNA molecule has two spirals called helixes.

DNA - See also: *Cells, Genes, Molecule.*

Doctors

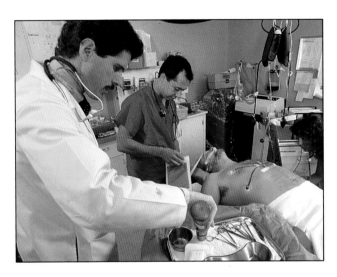

A doctor in the emergency unit of a hospital attending to a patient.

A doctor is a person who is trained to diagnose and treat disease. The title also describes people who have earned a doctorate degree in a subject like mathematics, language or philosophy.

Medical education probably first began in ancient Greece. In the fifth century BC Hippocrates devised the Hippocratic oath. This is a code of conduct for doctors which is still used today.

When a person has completed the training necessary to become a doctor, there are different fields of medicine that he or she can work in, such as general practice, or specialist areas such as pediatrics (the care of children), psychiatry or surgery.

Many doctors are also involved in preventive medicine, which concentrates on preventing conditions like heart disease or tooth decay.

Doctors - See also: *Dentistry, Hospitals, Medicine, Nursing, Pediatrics, Surgery.*

Dogs

Dogs are mammals with long jaws, and teeth that are well suited to eating flesh. They have five toes on each front foot and four toes on each hind foot. They have strong claws, which they cannot pull in as cats do.

Domestic dogs

Dogs were probably the first animals to be domesticated, perhaps before 10,000 BC, and they serve humans in many ways. They may be pets, or sporting dogs such as greyhounds, guard dogs such as dobermans, tracking dogs such as bloodhounds, working dogs such as sheep and cattle dogs, or dogs used for pulling sleds, such as the husky. It has taken a long time to breed dogs for these special purposes.

The wolf appears to be closely related to the domestic dog.

Wild dogs

There are many different wild dogs, including the Siberian wild dog, the Indian wild dog and the Cape hunting dog of Africa. The maned wolf, Cordillera fox and crab-eating fox live in South America. The coyote of North America has managed to survive even in areas settled by humans. The dingo is thought to have been brought to Australia by Aborigines, and was a domestic dog that became wild again.

Wolves

Wolves look like Alsatians, but are more powerful and have a longer nose, stronger jaws and a bushy tail that always hangs down. They often hunt in a pack, working in a team to attack animals stronger than themselves.

The she-wolf has her cubs in a den made of dried leaves, moss and hairs from her belly. She has from three to nine cubs, which are born blind. She cares for them until they are old enough to look after themselves. The father stays with the family and will bring up the cubs if anything happens to the mother.

Dd

Dogs

The dingo was domesticated by the Australian Aborigines, but has since returned to the wild.

The blue heeler (right) is an Australian dog bred to help herd cattle.

Foxes

Foxes have long bodies and short legs, pointed snouts, big ears and bushy tails. Foxes live in burrows called 'earths'. They usually live on small animals like insects or mice, but will sometimes eat chickens and lambs. They may even eat fish or fruit. Many foxes are hunted for their fur. In some places foxes are raised on fur farms.

Dogs - See also: *Domestic Animals, Feral Animals, Mammals, Nocturnal Animals.*

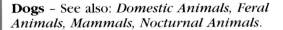

31

Dolphins

A dolphin is a small, toothed whale that lives in the sea. It is a mammal, not a fish. Mammals, unlike fish, feed their young on milk that is produced in the mother's body.

Dolphins breathe through lungs and are warm-blooded (that is, their body temperature stays fairly constant). Fish, on the other hand, breathe through gills.

Most dolphins live in sea water and remain near the land for most of their life. They prefer warm or tropical waters. They are closely related to porpoises, another group of sea mammals. The main differences between dolphins and porpoises are in their teeth and snout. Dolphins have a beaklike snout and cone-shaped teeth. Porpoises have a rounded snout and flat or spade-shaped teeth.

Dolphins range in size from 3 feet to 30 feet (1 meter to 9 meters). The largest dolphins are the killer whales. Bottle-nosed dolphins are the best known species.

They show great friendliness towards people, are easily trained, and adapt well to life in captivity.

All dolphins have a body shaped like a torpedo. This enables them to move through the water quickly. They have a pair of paddle-shaped flippers on their sides and a dorsal fin on their back. The fins help them to keep balance in the water. A powerful tail fin propels the dolphin through the water.

The skin of dolphins is smooth and rubbery. It contains a layer of fat to keep the animal warm. A dolphin breathes through a nostril on top of its head, called a blowhole. The blowhole is sealed by strong muscles while underwater.

Dolphins have a highly developed sense of hearing and good vision. They also have a natural sonar system called **echolocation**, which helps them locate objects underwater.

Bottle-nosed dolphins are intelligent and easily trained.

Dolphins – See also: *Fish, Mammals, Marine Animals, Whales.*

Dd

Domestic Animals

The dog may have been the first domesticated animal. Wild dogs probably stayed near camps and followed hunters, looking for food. Once they became tame, dogs were useful for guarding people and hunting. Some breeds, such as sheepdogs, huskies and bloodhounds, may still be used as working dogs, but many are now kept as pets.

Around 15,000 years ago, people followed wild herds of animals and hunted them for food. This changed about 10,000 years ago when sheep and goats began to be domesticated. People looked after domestic animals by taking them to places where there was food and protecting them from wild animals.

At first when people moved with their herds they walked, carrying all their belongings. After a while, animals such as horses and donkeys were domesticated and used for carrying loads.

When people began to grow plants for food, they could stop wandering with the animals and settle in villages. The ox and the onager, a kind of wild ass, were tamed and used to pull plows. When the wheel was invented, horses and oxen were trained to pull carts. People learned to ride horses about 2000 BC.

Goats were among the earliest animals to be domesticated.

Chickens are kept for their eggs and meat.

Camels are used as transport in desert countries.

The yak is a common beast of burden in the highlands of Tibet.

Kinds of domestic animals

Different animals were domesticated in different areas of the world. In Tibet, the yak carries loads, and provides milk, meat and hair. Even its dung is used as fuel for fires. In many parts of the world camels are an important domestic animal. The llama is still used as a pack animal in some parts of South America.

Reindeer are the only deer to have been really domesticated. They are used by people in cold, northern countries for meat, milk and skins. They are also used to pull sledges.

Elephants are sometimes trained to carry people and heavy loads. They can also pull and stack logs in forests.

Cats were domesticated more than 5,000 years ago, although they will go wild again very easily if they are not looked after. Cats have been very useful to humans because they kill rats and mice.

Domestic birds

Many species of birds have been domesticated, such as the red jungle fowl. It looks like a pheasant, but from it have come

 # D d

many kinds of domestic chickens. Other domestic birds include geese, ducks and peacocks.

The Egyptians kept pigeons for food, and probably to carry messages, as early as 3000 BC. Pigeons were important for carrying messages right up to World War II. Today pigeons are bred for meat, for racing, or to keep as pets.

Birds have probably been kept as pets in cages for thousands of years. Canaries were first brought to Europe from the Canary Islands in the 16th century. They used to be taken down coal mines, because they would die if poisonous gases were about, and so warn the miners to get out of the mine.

Elephants are used in many parts of the world to carry loads.

Domestic Animals – See also: *Beef Industry, Birds, Cats, Cattle, Dogs, Elephants, Feral Animals, Horses, Mammals.*

Clydesdale horses were bred as drafthorses, for farm work.

Drought

Cracked, dry earth during a drought in the Northern Territory of Australia.

Water is essential to all forms of life, but different species need different amounts of water to survive. Human beings need 7 to 9 pints (4 to 5 liters) of water each day to remain healthy.

A drought is a continuous period of little or no rain. As a result, the demand for water is greater than the amount available. In areas where rainfall is regular and reliable, excess water is usually stored in dams and reservoirs. In these areas droughts are rare. When there is a drought, it is usually short-lived, and is not a disaster. It may lead to the loss of crops and restrictions on the use of water reserves.

In other parts of the world where rainfall is irregular and unreliable, droughts can be major disasters. In many African countries farmers rely on annual rains for a successful harvest as there are few or no reserves of water. When there is no rain, especially for several years in a row, a drought occurs.

The first effect of a drought is crop failure. This means that food cannot be grown locally, and people go hungry. If the drought continues, famine on a massive scale may result. Thousands, or even millions, of people may starve to death.

Animals may also die from a lack of drinking water. If their usual plant food is not available, they may eat trees, shrubs and other plants, stripping the soil bare. This can lead to the fertile topsoil being blown away by the wind, turning farmland into desert.

At a local level, digging new wells helps to protect against minor droughts. On a larger scale, reservoirs can be built to store excess water in times of heavy rains.

Drought – See also: *Dam, Desert, Erosion, Land Degradation, Soil, Water Cycle, Water Supply*.

Dd

Drugs

A drug is any substance that affects how the body works. Some drugs, such as aspirin and cold medicines, are used to treat minor illnesses and can be bought over the counter at a pharmacy. Other drugs need to be prescribed by a doctor before a pharmacist will sell them to you. These drugs can be more dangerous than over-the-counter drugs if they are not used correctly.

For centuries, drugs have been made from animal and plant extracts. Now, many drugs are also made from synthetic substances.

Before a drug is given to the general public, it is carefully tested in the laboratory to see how it works. Then it is tested on laboratory animals to see if it is effective, what dose is needed and if there are side-effects. Finally it is tested on volunteer humans.

Drugs are given to patients in different ways depending on how the drug works in the body, and how quickly it must act. Intravenous injection, that is, the injection of a drug directly into a vein, is used when quick action is needed. Other drugs can be injected into the muscle, or just below the skin. Many drugs are given by mouth. Drugs with gas in them can be inhaled into the lungs. Skin diseases can be treated by applying creams that contain drugs directly to the skin.

Some drugs are used for pleasure, like alcohol, marijuana and cocaine. The use of some of these drugs is illegal because they can cause a loss of control, and the person using them can become dependent on them.

Drugs – See also: *Alcohol, Animals, Antibiotics, Penicillin, Vaccination.*

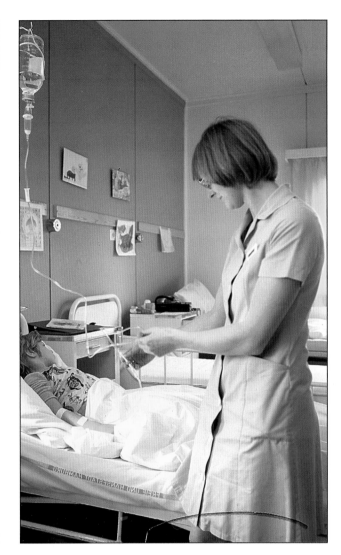

Drugs can be administered intravenously through a 'drip'.

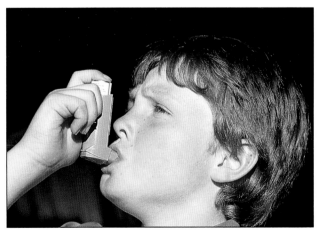

A child inhaling ventolin to relieve an asthma attack.

Dyes

Dyes are a group of chemical substances used to produce color in a fabric. They are sometimes referred to as colorants. They are usually made from chemicals extracted from coal tar and petroleum.

They are used by the textile industry to color fibers, yarns and fabrics. Manufacturers also use them to color foods, inks, leather, paper, plastics and wood.

Before dyes became available, fabrics were treated with natural colorants made from plants or even insects. The bright-red cochineal was made from the bodies of cochineal beetles.

The first artificial dye was made by English chemist William Perkin in the 1850s. His dye, mauveine, was made commercially. Over the next 100 years, the range of natural colors was replaced by a wider choice of synthetic dyes.

Fabric is dyed in steel or aluminium vats.

Early dyeing technology used wooden vats in which the material was stirred constantly in the dye solution. Stainless steel and aluminium have replaced timber and have made the process of industrial dyeing much faster.

Cochineal beetles, from which red dye can be made.

Dyes – See also: *Paints and Pigments, Textiles.*

Ears

The ears are organs of hearing and balance. The ear is made up of three parts: the outer, middle and inner ear. The outer ear is the only visible part. The rest of the ear is in the skull.

The outer ear collects sound waves from the air and sends them along the ear canal to the eardrum. This is a thin, tight membrane, like the surface of a drum. It vibrates when sound waves hit it.

The middle ear has three tiny bones which send the energy from the vibrations of the eardrum along to the inner ear. They also protect the ear from very intense sounds by reducing the size of the vibrations entering the inner ear.

The inner ear is made up of labyrinths. Within the labyrinth lies the cochlea, which is filled with liquid and lined with tiny hair-like cells. The vibrations from the middle ear make the liquid move, and the cells translate this motion into nervous impulses that go to the brain. The brain interprets this and recognizes the sound. The louder the sound, the more quickly nerve impulses are produced.

Deafness, which is partial or total loss of hearing, has several causes. Congenital deafness is when a baby is born with partial or total loss of hearing. Deafness can also be caused by damage to the nerve that carries impulses from the ear to the brain.

In less severe forms of deafness, the outer ear may have too much wax, which blocks the sound waves from entering the inner ear. The middle ear is connected to the mouth and

The parts of the ear.

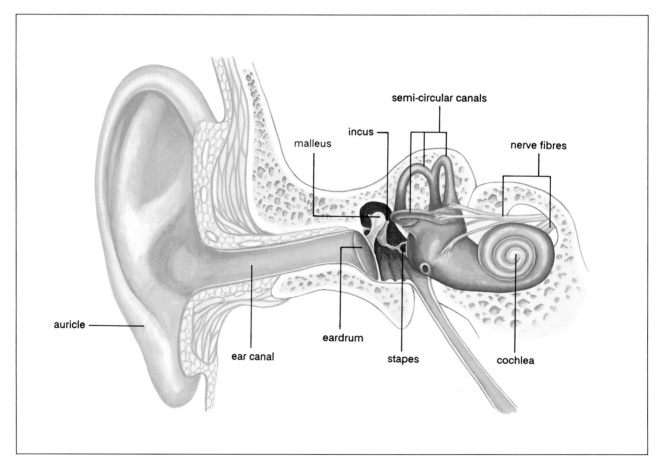

Modern hearing aids are very small machines that act as tiny amplifiers.

throat, and sometimes micro-organisms that enter the body through the nose or mouth can go into the middle ear and cause ear-ache, deafness or loss of balance.

Another cause of deafness is damage to the nerve that connects the ear to the brain. This can occur through injury, infection or exposure to very loud sounds.

Hearing aids increase the loudness of sound, and can help with deafness. Sometimes deafness can be cured by an operation on the inner ear.

Ears are also responsible for balance. A person's sense of balance can be affected by infection in the fluid in the ear canals, or when rapid movements confuse the messages being sent to the brain. The loss of a sense of balance causes a person to become dizzy.

Ears - See also: *Brain, Senses, Sound, Speech.*

Earth

The Earth is one of nine planets which, together with the Sun, form our solar system. It is the third planet from the Sun and the fifth largest planet in the solar system.

The Earth is about 4,500 million years old. It formed with the rest of the solar system as a cloud of dust and gas. For millions of years it was in a hot, molten state. As it cooled, a rocky crust formed across its surface. This outer layer is called the crust or lithosphere. Its depth varies from 6 to 19 miles (10 to 30 kilometers). Beneath the lithosphere is the mantle which is also made of rock. It is about 1,800 miles (2,900 kilometers) thick. Next is the outer core consisting of liquid iron. Then, in the center is the inner core which is a huge ball of solid iron. Its diameter is about 1,550 miles (2,500 kilometers). The center is extremely hot — 10,800°F (6,000°C).

The crust of the Earth is made up of gigantic plates, which float on the heavier rocks of the mantle. The continents sit on top of these plates. As the plates move, the continents occasionally collide, and their rocks buckle to form mountains or break to form faults. All this movement occurs very slowly, over millions of years.

It takes one year, or 365¼ days, for the Earth to orbit the Sun. This means that every fourth year has an extra day (February 29) — which makes up for the quarter days. This type of year is called a leap year.

As well as traveling around the Sun, the Earth rotates on its axis (an imaginary line running from the North Pole to the South Pole). It takes 24 hours (one day) to complete one rotation. Most parts of the Earth experience a period of light and one of dark during this time.

The Earth surrounded by clouds, with the ice sheet covering Antarctica at the bottom.

Seasons

The Earth's axis is tilted at 23½°. This means that the Sun shines down on different places at different times of the year. For half the year the Sun is positioned over the **Northern Hemisphere**. During this period it is summer in the Northern Hemisphere and winter in the **Southern Hemisphere**. For the other half of the year the Sun is positioned over the Southern Hemisphere. During this time it is summer in the Southern Hemisphere and winter in the Northern Hemisphere.

Twice a year, on March 21 and September 23, the Sun is directly over the Equator. On these dates the day and the night are of equal length in all parts of the world.

As the Sun moves into one hemisphere or the other, the number of daylight hours increases, as does the amount of heat reaching the Earth's surface in that hemisphere. Quite simply, that hemisphere becomes warmer while the other becomes cooler.

Weather and climate

Surrounding the Earth is the **atmosphere**. It is made up of a mixture of gases that enables life to exist. It traps heat from the Sun and warms the Earth. The Earth would freeze if the atmosphere did not exist. It is in the lower part of the atmosphere that the weather systems of the world form.

The Earth is divided into different climatic regions. The warm tropics lie either side of the **equator**. The cooler temperate regions lie beyond the **Tropic of Cancer** and **Tropic of Capricorn**. At the north and south ends of the globe are the cold polar regions.

Life on Earth

Life began in the oceans more than three billion years ago. The first forms of life were single-celled organisms. These evolved into the huge variety of complex plants and animals that exist today. The Earth provides living things with air, food and water on which to survive. This is a carefully balanced system. It can become unbalanced if humans over-use the soil, and pollute the water and air.

The layers of the Earth.

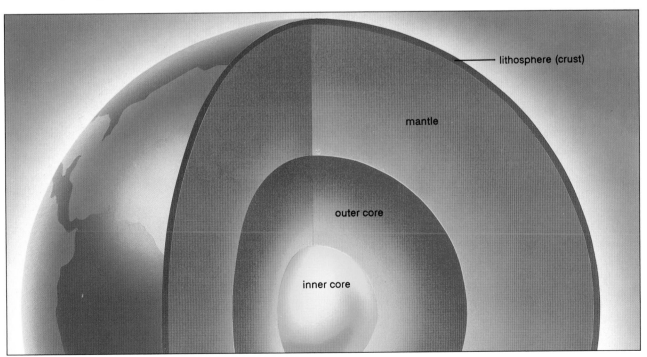

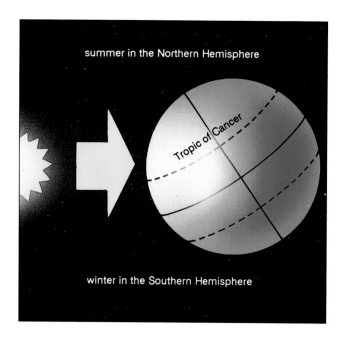

summer in the Northern Hemisphere

Tropic of Cancer

winter in the Southern Hemisphere

The position of the Earth on December 22.

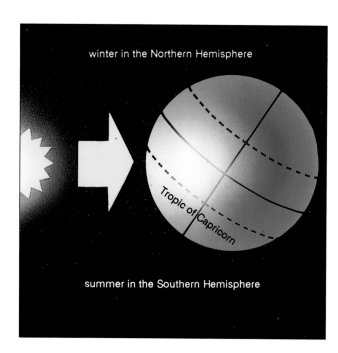

winter in the Northern Hemisphere

Tropic of Capricorn

summer in the Southern Hemisphere

The position of the Earth on June 21.

Earth - See also: *Atmosphere, Continent, Day and Night, Earthquake, Ecosystem, Evolution, Faulting and Folding, Hemisphere, Latitude and Longitude, Northern and Southern Lights, Oceans and Seas, Ozone Layer, Planets, Solar System, Sun, Weather.*

Earthquake

An earthquake is a sudden, often violent, movement of the Earth's surface. Most earthquakes occur along the edges of the continental plates that are part of the Earth's crust. These plates are not fixed; they move very slowly in different directions.

As two plates move past each other, they tend to lock together at the edges. As the rest of the plate continues to drift, enormous pressure builds up at the edge. Eventually this pressure causes the plates to slip suddenly. They may slip horizontally, vertically or in both directions. The movement can range from an inch or so to several feet. It creates shock waves that travel through the earth. These can cause huge cracks to open up in the ground.

Most of the world's earthquakes occur around the edge of the Pacific basin. One of

An earthquake fault line in New Zealand. The quake measured 6.25 on the Richter scale.

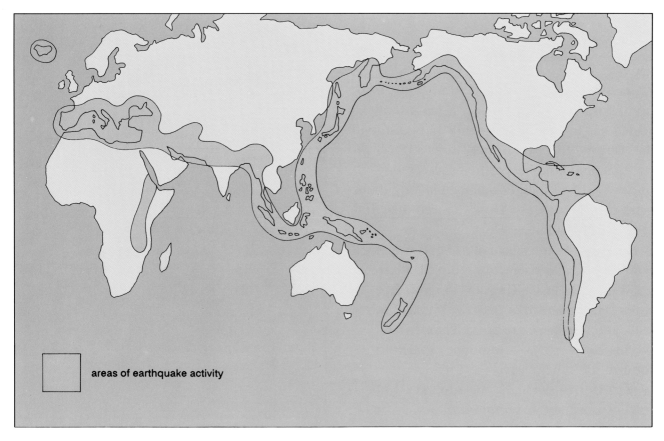

The major areas where earthquakes occur around the world.

areas of earthquake activity

the best-known earthquake regions is in California, in the United States. The San Andreas Fault is the line of contact between the North American plate, which is drifting slowly westward, and the Pacific plate, which is drifting north. There have been several large earthquakes in California in recent years.

Minor earthquakes, or tremors, are a common occurrence. There are about 20 small earthquakes each day in Japan. Major earthquakes are less common. Often they occur in isolated areas or under the sea. Large underwater earthquakes cause giant waves to form. These waves, known as tsunami, can be very destructive.

The strength of an earthquake is measured on the Richter scale. Zero is the weakest shock; nine is a major earthquake that can cause terrible damage. The strongest earthquake was recorded in Chile in 1960. It measured 8.9 on the Richter scale.

Earthquake – See also: *Continent, Earth, Faulting and Folding.*

Earthworms

An earthworm has a long, flexible body, made up of parts called 'segments'. It has a thin skin which has to be kept moist, or the worm will die. Earthworms live in moist soils all over the world. Some kinds of earthworms are tiny, under $\frac{1}{32}$ of an inch (a millimeter) long, but giant earthworms can grow to more than 10 feet (3 meters) long.

Earthworms are sensitive to light, touch, temperature and chemicals. They also have a good sense of taste. They are **hermaphrodites**. This means that each worm has both male and female sex organs. When two worms mate, each one produces sperm to fertilize the other's eggs.

Earthworms are night animals and do not usually move above ground during the day. They make burrows in the ground, swallowing earth as they go. As soil passes through the worm, it is ground up in the worm's gizzard. Rotting plant or animal matter in the soil is digested. Anything that the

Castings left by an earthworm.

earthworm cannot digest is left on the surface of the ground as **castings**.

In moist and rainy weather the worms live near the surface. In cold weather, or in very hot, dry weather, they plug the opening of the burrow and stay in its deepest part.

Earthworms are important because their burrows allow air to flow through the soil. The worms also help to mix and break up the soil as they tunnel through it.

An earthworm's body is made up of segments.

Earthworms - See also: *Food Chain.*

Echo

An echo is the sound that we hear after it is reflected off a wall or building. When we make a loud noise, sound waves travel through the air in all directions. The first sound that we hear in our ears is the sound that travels from the source directly into our ears. Some of the sound waves will hit a distant wall or building and bounce back. When the reflected sound waves reach our ears, we again hear the sound. It may take a few seconds before the reflected wave reaches our ear. This is because, in air, sound travels at about 1,115 feet (340 meters) per second.

We do not hear an echo in all situations. Sometimes the reflected sound is too weak or the distant object is too far away or too small. Sometimes we hear more than one echo. Such repeated echoing is common in valleys and canyons where there are many reflections.

The sound waves bounce from wall to wall, producing several echoes.

Sailors use echo sounders (sonars) to measure the depth of seas or rivers or to locate a school of fish. Echo sounders are attached to the underside of ships. They send out a series of blips in any direction. The speed of sound in water is 4,725 feet (1,440 meters) per second. The time it takes for sound to travel out and return to the ship allows the depth to be measured accurately within 1 foot (30 centimeters). Echoes are reflected back to a tuned receiver as audible beeps. A skilled operator can tell from the sound what sort of object the sound bounced off.

Bats and dolphins also use echoes to locate objects.

Today, computers analyze underwater conditions accurately to within an eighth of an inch (a few millimeters). They can pinpoint such objects as hidden reefs, icebergs and sunken ships.

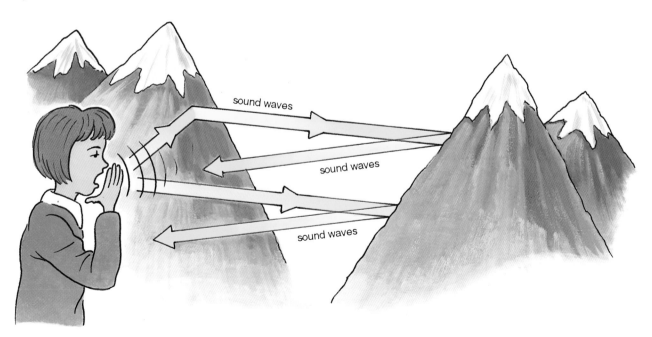

When sound waves bounce from mountain to mountain, we hear more than one echo.

Echo - See also: *Dolphins, Fishing Industry, Nocturnal Animals, Sonar, Sound.*

Eclipse

An eclipse occurs when one heavenly body blocks out the light of another. On Earth we see two types of eclipses: lunar and solar. These occur when the Sun, Moon and Earth are in a line.

When the Earth is between the Sun and the Moon, the Earth's shadow falls on the Moon, robbing the Moon of light. This is a **lunar eclipse**. A total lunar eclipse is when the Moon is completely in the Earth's shadow. A partial lunar eclipse is when only part of the Moon is in the Earth's shadow. There are about 155 lunar eclipses every 100 years.

When the Moon comes directly between the Sun and the Earth, it blocks out the light from the Sun. This is a **solar eclipse**. A total solar eclipse is when the Moon blocks out the Sun completely. When this happens, day becomes night for a short time. Total solar eclipses are rare events.

A partial solar eclipse occurs when the Moon blocks only part of the Sun. These are the more common type of solar eclipse.

Sometimes the Moon appears smaller in the sky than the Sun (when it is at its furthest from Earth). If a solar eclipse happens at this time, the outer ring of the Sun can be seen around the edge of the dark Moon. This is known as an annular eclipse.

It is dangerous to look at the Sun at any time, even during a solar eclipse.

A solar eclipse occurs when the moon blocks out light from the Sun.

Eclipse - See also: *Moon, Sun.*

Ecosystem

Every living thing depends on its environment and other living things for survival. **Ecology** is the study of how living things interact with each other and their environments.

An **ecosystem** is an environment that provides plants and animals with the things they need to survive, including food, water, shelter, space and light. The Earth itself is a huge ecosystem. Within it many smaller ecosystems can be identified, such as forest, desert and marine ecosystems.

A forest, for example, is the perfect habitat for many animals, from large mammals such as deer, to birds and tiny insects. In return, these animals play a part in maintaining the forest. Trees provide shelter for birds and other animals, as well as food in the form of fruit. When a bird eats the fruit, the seeds often pass through it unharmed. As the bird flies, the seeds are transported to another part of the forest and are returned to the forest floor in the bird's droppings. These seeds will then grow into new trees to replace dead or dying trees.

In this ecosystem the bird benefits from eating the tree's fruit, and the tree also benefits. Together the trees and birds ensure the continuation of the ecosystem. If either the trees or the birds were to disappear, the entire ecosystem might collapse.

Human activities such as logging and pollution can upset this balance, destroying or damaging ecosystems. However, humans also require healthy ecosystems to survive. It is in our interests to make sure the balance is maintained.

> **Ecosystem** – See also: *Biodiversity, Environmental Care, Food Chain, Forests, Habitat, Plants, Pollution.*

A tropical rainforest ecosystem. Each living thing depends on other living things to survive.

Egg

Most animals produce eggs as a way of producing young. However, only certain animals, such as birds, force eggs out of their body.

Young can only develop from fertilized eggs. In most mammals, the fertilized egg is small and stays inside the female's body. The young mammal develops from the egg. Over time, the young grows into an animal resembling its parents.

Birds' eggs vary greatly in size, shape and color. The largest birds usually lay the largest eggs. The largest egg is that of the ostrich. The number of eggs laid at one time also varies from species to species. Hens and ducks can lay up to 350 eggs per year. Gulls lay only about four eggs per year.

Most wild birds lay their eggs in nests of straw, grass or sticks. Some lay eggs on rocks and some bury their eggs in the sand. Eggs are also laid by insects, fish, amphibians and reptiles. Eggs laid by chickens are used by humans as a source of food.

Egg – See also: *Amphibians, Birds, Fish, Mammals, Metamorphosis, Reproductive System, Reptiles.*

Birds' egg vary in size and color. Eggs that are laid in exposed places often have protective coloration such as spots that blend in with the environment.

Electricity

Electricity has become the most important source of energy in the world. We cannot see electricity but we do know what it does. When we turn on an electric light, we can see light and we can feel the bulb getting hot. Electricity enables us to operate such things as televisions, computers and dishwashers. Lightning is a natural flash of light caused by electricity in the atmosphere.

Most of the electricity around us is due to a flow of tiny particles called **electrons**. These exist inside atoms. Atoms are particles that make up every substance around us. Electrons are too small to be seen even with a microscope.

When we turn on an electric light switch in our homes, electrons flow through the switch and the wires connected to it. A flow of electrons is called an electric current.

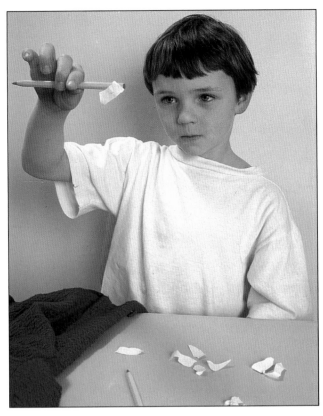

To create an electrical charge, rub a
plastic pen with a piece of wool. The pen
will then attract paper, above, and
attract or deflect water, below.

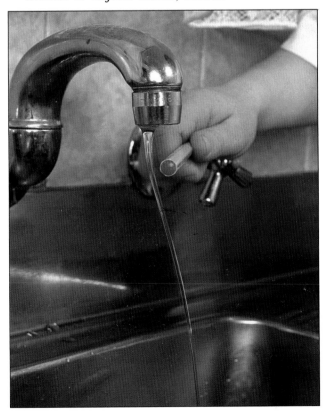

Electrons have a certain amount of energy.
When they pass through a light bulb, they
give up some or all of their energy to produce
light. When electrons pass through a toaster,
they produce heat. When you turn on a
flashlight, electricity is produced from
chemicals inside the batteries.

Electricity that flows through wires is called
current electricity. Current electricity is
produced by batteries or generators.

There is another type of electricity, called
static electricity. You can generate static
electricity by rubbing a plastic comb through
dry hair. The hair loses electrons and these
stick to the comb. The static electricity makes
the hair crackle as you comb it. If you remove
a nylon shirt in the dark, you can sometimes
see flashes of light and hear sparks.
Sometimes you feel a shock or spark as you
touch a metal door knob after walking on
nylon carpet. These events are caused by
static electricity. This type of electricity is
called static because the electric charges are
not free to flow; they simply remain stationary
on the surface of the object.

Discovery

During the 1700s, there were many devices
made for producing electricity. Most were
involved with static electricity. In 1752
American scientist Benjamin Franklin
conducted his famous kite and key
experiment during a thunderstorm. He
discovered the connection between electricity
and lightning.

In 1821 British scientist Michael Faraday
demonstrated the world's first electric motor.
In 1831 he showed how this could be used to
create a small electric generator. Joseph
Henry, working on his own in the United
States, made the same discovery in the same
year.

Over the next 20 years various types of
industrial machinery were adapted for running

on batteries. The first major use of electricity came during the 1840s when a large generator was built for use in a factory.

During the mid 1800s a number of inventors tried to develop the electric light. Several were made but they did not last long. In 1879, Thomas Edison worked out a way of making an electric light last for a long period of time. He had problems finding the right material to use as a filament. He finally succeeded with a carbonized thread of cotton. He prevented it from burning out by drawing out all the air from inside the bulb. The globe became known as the incandescent light bulb.

High-voltage transmission lines are supported by steel or concrete towers, and carry power long distances.

Electricity – See also: *Atom, Battery, Energy, Hydroelectric Power, Magnetic Energy, Nuclear Energy, Power Stations, Solar Energy, Thunder and Lightning, Water Energy, Wind Energy.*

Electronics

Electrons are electrically charged parts of an atom. A flow of electrons through a substance or wire is called an electric current. Electronics is the control of electron flow inside vacuum tubes, transistors, silicon chips and integrated circuits. The control of electrons allows us to produce a wide range of 'electronic' devices. These include lasers, microwave ovens, television sets and computers. Electronics is one of the most important sciences in the modern world.

Electronics and electricity both deal with electric current, but each focuses on a different use of current. Electricity deals with current as a form of energy that can be used to power lights, heaters, motors and other

Part of the electronic circuit board of a computer disc drive.

equipment. Electronics treats current as a means of carrying information. Currents that carry information are called **signals**. The signals in electronic circuits are classified as **analog** or **digital**. An analog signal can have any value within a certain range. Digital signals are a bit like a switch — either on or off. Computers are the main users of digital signals. Analog signals are used to represent sounds and pictures in televisions.

Electronic devices such as hi-fi systems, tape recorders and computers work on an input signal, a processor and an output signal. The input can be a microphone and the output can be a loudspeaker. The processor consists of an electronic amplifying circuit to control what happens to the input signal. Amplification is a strengthening of a weak electric signal. It is the most basic and important electronic function. Most electronic equipment could not work without a fast, efficient means of amplification. A device that does this is called an **amplifier**.

Much of the recent development work in electronics has been devoted to making even smaller devices and complex integrated circuits.

Electronics - See also: *Atom, Computer Technology, Electricity, Fiber Optics, Household Appliances, Laser, Music, Silicon Chip, Technology, Television, Transistor.*

Elephants

Elephants are mammals. There are two kinds of elephant, the **African** and the **Indian**. A male African elephant may be over 10 feet (3 meters) high at the shoulder, and weigh around 6 tons (6 tonnes). Indian elephants are smaller, but live longer, up to 70 years.

Elephants have tiny eyes, but very large ears. To protect their very sensitive skins, elephants bathe often, roll in the mud and cover themselves with dust. They are intelligent and have a good memory. They use their trunks to touch and smell, and also to pick up things, including food and water.

A mother elephant is pregnant for 20 months before her young is born. Usually,

An African elephant.

An Indian elephant.

only one baby elephant is born at a time. They can walk two days after being born. Young elephants stay near their mothers, and other female elephants help to look after them. The adult males tend to live alone or in small groups with other males.

A herd may be made up of several elephant families. An old female usually leads the herd. If one of the herd is in trouble or hurt, others will help it. The older elephants use their tusks to protect the young ones from large cats such as lions. The tusks are large teeth made of ivory.

Elephants need a great deal of food and water. When feeding, they strip bark off trees and break branches. They are always on the move looking for food, and they migrate in search of new feeding grounds.

There are far fewer elephants than there used to be. Many have been killed for their ivory tusks. In spite of laws limiting the numbers of elephants that can be killed, illegal killing still goes on. Also, as more land is used by people for farming, there is less space for elephants to live in.

Elephants - See also: *Domestic Animals, Endangered Animals, Mammals, Migration, Prehistoric Animals.*

Emergency Services

Emergency services are involved in rescuing people from hazardous situations, such as floods, accidents or fires. Such services need an efficient system of communication and specialized machinery. Many emergency services are linked up to large buildings such as skyscrapers and airports. Because large numbers of people are present at such locations, it is important that any emergency is attended to quickly. Alarms automatically go off in fire or police stations whenever something goes wrong. Even small buildings that contain dangerous chemicals or other materials have systems that automatically alert the emergency services when a dangerous situation develops. Many cities have security systems that monitor the condition of important or harzardous buildings.

Rescuing stranded sailors or plane crash survivors at sea is done by lifeboat or helicopter, or both. Ships in distress usually have automatic beacons that send out an SOS signal. There are also specially reserved radio-telephone channels that are used by crew on

Some private boating clubs have their own emergency services. This lifeboat went to the rescue when the sailboat's rudder broke.

the distressed ship. Many life jackets have automatic emergency beacons fitted to them as well.

Helicopters are often used for rescue at sea because they are much faster than lifeboats and can cover a wider area. They are fitted with many of the same detection devices carried by the lifeboats. Some helicopters are equipped as airborne hospitals. They are capable of giving people emergency treatment between accident sites and the main hospital.

A Sikorsky Sea King rescue helicopter can lift four people to safety at once.

Emergency Services - See also: *Fire-fighting, Helicopter.*

Endangered Animals

Extinction has occurred when there are no animals of a particular species (or type) left living. Once an animal species is extinct, it is gone forever. A species which is under threat of extinction is said to be endangered.

Before the 18th century, the world's human population grew fairly slowly. It is estimated that one animal species became extinct every 100 years. This was a result of natural causes such as changes in climate and plant life, and diseases.

The whaling industry has caused many species to become endangered.

The Australian bilby (above).

Once the human population began to grow more rapidly, animals became extinct at a faster rate. In the past 300 years nearly 80 species of birds have become extinct.

Some animals became extinct because they lived in only a small area, such as on an island, and were not used to being hunted. The dodo and the great auk are two birds that became extinct because they could not fly and were easily hunted. In New Zealand another flightless bird, the moa, was also hunted, first by the Maori and later by European sealers. Rats and other introduced animals brought to New Zealand ate the moa's eggs.

Today many species of animals are in danger of extinction as a result of human activities. The growing human population has meant that natural environments have been destroyed to make way for farming, mining and housing. Forests are cut down, swamps are drained, bushland is used for cattle grazing. When this happens, the plant and animal species that live in that environment lose their home, and disappear. In Madagascar 21 species of lemurs are facing extinction because the forests in which they live are being chopped down. In Australia the bilby, a small marsupial, is now endangered because introduced rabbits and cattle have taken over much of its habitat.

The trade in animal furs has led to some animals becoming endangered. Animals such as the fox, marten, otter and sable have been trapped, poisoned and shot to provide furs for coats. The snow leopard of Asia has also been hunted for its beautiful spotted coat and is now extremely rare.

The Asian lion was brought close to extinction in the 19th century when it was hunted for sport. Other species, such as whales, are hunted for profit. Large numbers of whales were slaughtered for meat, pet food, oil and whalebone. Whaling brought five species close to extinction until laws were introduced to save them. However, some whale hunting continues today.

The gorillas of Africa have become endangered partly because of poachers who killed them to sell their body parts as tourist souvenirs.

The snow leopard has been hunted for its fur.

A pile of skins from illegally killed ocelots, jaguars and margays.

Endangered animals are often protected by laws, or bred in zoos and special reserves to try to save them from extinction. If the breeding program is successful, some of these animals can be returned to their natural habitat. Unfortunately, rare animals can often be sold to collectors for very high prices, and this encourages poachers to trap them illegally.

Endangered Animals - See also: *Cats, Conservation, Environmental Care, Extinction, Flightless Birds, Feral Animals, Food Chain, Habitat, Mammals, Marsupials, Primates, Seals, Whales, Zoos.*

Energy

Energy is the ability of something to do work. For example, work is done whenever a force moves something a distance. Energy comes in different forms and exists in different situations. Energy is never created nor destroyed but always changes from one form to another.

There are two main types of energy: potential and kinetic. **Potential energy** is shown by a spring that is wound up ready to unwind, or a brand new car battery that is waiting to start a car. Another example of potential energy is an object held high above the Earth's surface. Because of gravity, this object has the potential to fall quickly. A dam full of water, built high in the mountains, has potential energy. When the water flows from the dam to a lower level it releases its potential energy. The flowing water can be used to turn turbines and generate electricity. This is the principle of hydro-electric power stations.

Kinetic energy is the energy that allows the movement of an object. The larger the object and the faster it is moving the more kinetic energy it has. A very large truck traveling at 30 miles (48 kilometers) per hour has a lot of kinetic energy. The same truck traveling at 10 miles (16 kilometers) per hour has less kinetic energy. Water flowing down a

Oil is piped across land for use in homes and factories. This pipeline is in Alaska.

hill into a power station has kinetic energy. The power station converts this energy into electricity.

Solar energy

All energy on Earth originally came from the Sun. It travels through space and reaches the Earth where it heats up the air, water and land. This type of energy is called solar energy. It reaches our planet every day. We are able to use it to dry clothes, heat water and cook food. Recently the technology for converting the Sun's rays to electricity has been developed. Solar cells are devices that convert sunlight into electricity. The development of panels of solar cells has enabled remote places to receive electricity.

Electrical energy

Electricity is a form of energy. Most electricity comes from power stations that burn coal or gas to turn water into steam. The steam is used to turn large generators. Electricity can also be produced from batteries, wind generators and solar cells. All of these sources have stored energy that is converted into kinetic energy in order to provide electricity for our daily needs. Electrical energy is also contained in lightning.

Chemical energy

Chemical energy is stored inside many fuels such as petroleum, coal, natural gas and wood. These fuels can be burned to give off energy that we can use. Chemical energy is

Solar cells can be mounted on a solar panel to convert sunlight into electrical energy.

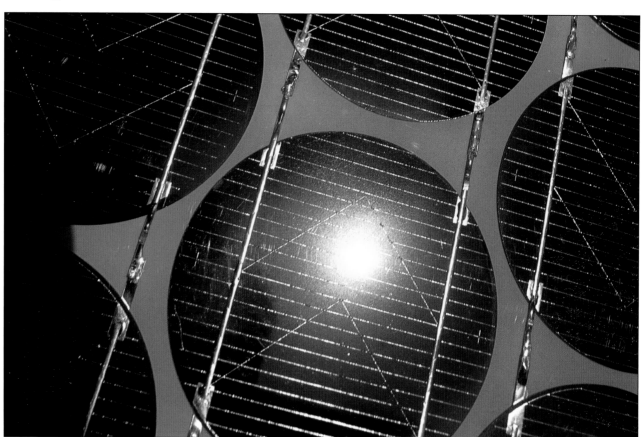

also found in the food we eat. Batteries also contain chemical energy. When a battery is used, chemical energy is converted into electrical energy.

Wave energy

Waves carry a lot of energy. Devices have been made to convert wave power into electricity. Tidal power stations have been built on the coasts of some countries. These use the power of tides to produce electricity.

Sound waves also carry energy. When sound waves strike our eardrums the eardrum vibrates backwards and forwards.

Wind energy

Moving air, or wind, is a potential source of large amounts of energy. The force of wind can uproot trees and move seeds and small animals thousands of miles.

Wind energy is a clean and renewable energy source. Large windmills connected to generators can be used to produce electricity in areas that are usually very windy.

Light and heat energy

Light and heat energy are usually closely related. The greatest source of light and heat is the Sun. A light bulb converts electrical energy to light and heat.

Nuclear energy

In the 1930s scientists discovered that the atom was a source of immense energy. When the atom is split, much energy is released. This can be seen in the power of an atomic bomb. In a nuclear power station, atomic reactions are carefully controlled and energy is released at a steady rate. The heat from the reaction is used to convert water into steam. The steam is then used to turn electricity generators.

Windmills can be used to pump water or generate electricity.

Energy - See also: *Chemical Energy, Fuel, Geothermal Energy, Hydroelectric Power, Magnetic Energy, Natural Gas, Natural Resources, Nuclear Energy, Power Stations, Radiant Energy, Water Energy, Wind Energy.*

Engine

An engine is a machine that does mechanical work. The energy that drives the machine comes from heat created by the burning of fuels such as coal or gasoline. There are two main types of engines — internal combustion, such as the car engine, and external combustion, such as the steam engine. All engines convert heat energy into mechanical energy so that work can be done.

External combustion engine

In the piston steam engine, heat generated outside the engine's working parts is used to turn water into steam. The steam then pushes the engine's pistons back and forth. When connected to a flywheel, the action of the pistons can be made to turn something.

The modern steam engine was invented by James Watt in 1791. Steam engines provided the technology that started the Industrial Revolution. During the 19th century, steam engines were used to power almost every kind of machine, from small factory engines to giant steam ships, from cars to locomotives.

James Watt's steam engine in 1791.

Internal combustion engine

Later in the 19th century, the internal combustion engine was developed as an alternative to steam. It is called an internal combustion engine because the fuel is burned inside the engine's working parts. The first successful gas engine was built in 1859 by Jean Lenoir in Paris. This invention was soon followed by the more successful Otto gas engines, designed by Nikolaus Otto. Gas engines were cheaper than steam engines. With the development of petroleum as a fuel, the internal combustion engine began to develop as a serious form of power.

The invention of the carburetor helped advance internal combustion engines. The carburetor is a device that controls the flow of gasoline and air into the engine's cylinders. A mixture of gasoline and air is squirted into each cylinder and ignited by a spark from a spark plug. The resulting explosion forces a piston to move. Each movement of the piston up and down the cylinder between explosions is called a 'stroke'. The typical car engine is a 'four-stroke' engine. A rod connected to the lower end of the piston turns a crankshaft.

In a typical car engine there are four to eight cylinders, each with a piston. The crankshaft is connected to the flywheel that drives the axles and wheels of the car.

The internal combustion engine and frame of a 1913 Model T Ford.

The diesel engine is a heavier version of the internal combustion engine. It uses high pressure to heat and ignite the fuel, which is heavier than the gasoline used in normal car engines. To provide the pressure, the diesel engine needs to be bigger and heavier. For this reason they are used mainly in larger vehicles, such as trucks, buses and boats.

The jet engine makes the internal combustion engine more efficient and more powerful. In a jet engine there are rows of blades that are driven by the igniting of the fuel. The ignition takes place in a central shaft and the power of the explosion is forced out through the layers of blades.

A modern internal combustion engine being lowered into place in a car.

Engine - See also: *Airplanes, Car, Oil, Road Transport.*

Engineering

Engineering is a science that involves designing structures, machines, and products of all kinds. An engineer uses knowledge of the physical sciences and mathematics to develop devices of practical use. Engineers are closely related to technologists.

Although engineering is associated with science, there are some differences. Science tends to be more involved with research into questions about space, energy and atomic physics. Engineering is about making use of the answers to these questions and solving technical and industrial problems.

The concept of engineering can be traced back to the beginnings of civilization since people have always been designing and building things of practical use.

Civil engineering includes such activities as the construction of bridges, roads and buildings. It requires a knowledge of soil structure, water flow, transportation, waste treatment and building structure.

Aerospace engineering involves the design, construction and maintenance of commercial and military aircraft, such as helicopters, airplanes, spacecraft and missiles. Aircraft have to be built as light as possible, with maximum strength.

Nuclear engineering is concerned with the design, construction and maintenance of nuclear power stations.

Electrical engineers design and supervise the building of equipment that supplies electricity for domestic and industrial consumption. Electronic engineering involves the design of micro-circuits and silicon chips.

Mechanical engineering involves the design and building of all sorts of machines, including trains, motor cars, power plants for industry, and robotics.

Chemical engineering is the manufacture of

An engineer using a computer to help design a building.

everyday consumer items involving chemical processes.

Today, new fields of engineering are emerging as a result of new scientific and technological discoveries.

Engineering – See also: *Airplanes, Building Industry, Electronics, Nuclear Energy, Physics, Silicon Chip, Technology.*